BE KIND

BE KIND

A 52-Week Journal for Practicing Kindness

HOUSTON KRAFT

SIMON ELEMENT

New York   London   Toronto   Sydney   New Delhi

SIMON
ELEMENT

An Imprint of Simon & Schuster, Inc.
1230 Avenue of the Americas
New York, NY 10020

First Simon Element trade paperback edition September 2023

SIMON ELEMENT is a trademark of Simon & Schuster, Inc.

For information about special discounts for bulk purchases,
please contact Simon & Schuster Special Sales at 1-866-506-1949
or business@simonandschuster.com.

The Simon & Schuster Speakers Bureau can bring authors to your live event.
For more information or to book an event, contact the
Simon & Schuster Speakers Bureau at 1-866-248-3049
or visit our website at www.simonspeakers.com.

Manufactured in the United States of America

1   3   5   7   9   10   8   6   4   2

Library of Congress Cataloging-in-Publication Data has been applied for.

ISBN 978-1-6680-2759-2
ISBN 978-1-6680-2760-8 (ebook)

TABLE OF CONTENTS

52 x 1 x 10

52 weeks

1 person per week

10 minutes of Deep Kindness

THE PRACTICE OF KINDNESS

I was walking through the halls of a high school campus I was speaking at when I saw a poster that read, "Throw Kindness around like confetti." It was not the first time I'd seen this saying—I've come across it in social media posts, on T-shirts, and in various school hallways—but for some reason, this encounter felt different.

Perhaps it was some particularly negative news cycle. Maybe the moment was painted by the students who had just confided in me about some horrific situation they were dealing with at home. Whatever the reason, I felt anger looking at this piece of paper in the fluorescent ninth-grade hallway.

Kindness, I thought, *is much more complicated than confetti.*

Right out of college, I started presenting in schools as a motivational speaker. I believe in the power of storytelling and connection and wanted to share a message about Kindness and hope. Over the course of about seven years, this adventure took me to around six hundred campuses all over the world.

Nearly every place I visited had some sort of motto or mission statement related to Kindness. Posters about being Kind exist in just about every school I've spoken at. None of them, I realized as I unpacked my poster-based frustration, talked about Kindness in a way that honored how hard it is.

I believe one of the most damaging narratives our culture offers us is the idea that Kindness is simple. Or easy. Or free.

Kindness is never free. It always costs us *something*. At the bare minimum, the practice of Kindness costs us time. Time spent reflecting or preparing to act thoughtfully. Time listening or empathizing. Time to hold the door open as someone else walks through or time to prepare a meal for someone who is sick.

It also costs us attention. The world competes for our attention every day, which is why when we *pay* attention, we must consider the amount we are paying. To give Kindness is to give our attention to a person, or a pursuit.

Kindness, as the practice gets deeper and more meaningful, costs us more complicated things like comfort or pride. Compassion often requires actions that inconvenience or challenge us. We must pursue choices that exercise vulnerability or humility or courage. Kindness asks us to see beyond the present messy moment or our naturally selfish selves toward a more beneficial future.

Kindness is not confetti. It is not simply a random act.

The author Will Durant once mused, "We are what we repeatedly do. Excellence, then, is not an act but a habit." John Addison says, "We are not human beings, we are human becomings." I believe if we want to *be* something like Kind, we have to *become* it. To *become* anything, we must repeatedly *do* it.

That's why this journal is not a series of random acts. It is a practice. A deliberate, consistent pursuit of becoming the kind of Kind person I believe we all hope to be. And, by doing so, adding to the collective Kindness of a world in desperate need of more of it.

Did you know that forty-five percent of our day is built on routine? If you extend the premise, that means that forty-five percent of our week is habitual. When you really consider it, about half our life is just a series of habits. What if we added a weekly routine of Kindness to that forty-five percent? What might it look like to make Kindness a routine instead of a random act?

Charles Duhigg, in his book *The Power of Habit*, shares that most habits are created with the same three ingredients: a cue, a routine, and a reward. When we experience a cue (we get home from school or work; we see the fridge; our alarm goes off at 4 p.m.), it begins a routine (we sit down on the couch and turn on the TV; we rummage through the leftovers; we put on our workout clothes). The routine is motivated by a reward (we get to turn our brains off; we get a quick sugar spike; we feel accomplished getting out the door to the gym).

In order to create a thoughtful habit related to compassion that sticks around, you have to get serious about your own cue, routine, and reward. What if, just one day a week, the first thing you dedicated your morning to was Kindness? You keep this bad boy next to your bed and, right when you wake up (cue), you spend a few moments reflecting and putting Kindness into action (routine). The very first choice of your day is to reflect on amazing humans and do good for you and the world (reward).

Then, before you get under the covers at night (cue), you reflect on your day and your moment of Kindness (routine). The final thing you do before bed is think about the positivity in the world that you created or wanted to create that day (reward).

The ways that we could practice are bountiful and beautiful. To keep us focused over the course of this journal, the invitations to exercise Kindness will be focused on one person at a time. Each act can be completed in around ten minutes and will cost no money (unless you choose). The recommended frequency is once per week (ideally on a consistent day).

THINK OF IT LIKE THIS: 52 X 1 X 10

52 = 52 weeks

1 = 1 person a week

10 = An act of Kindness in 10 minutes or less

STEP-BY-STEP

1. Choose one day a week that you will consistently use this journal:

    M   T   W   Th   F   Sa   Su

2. On the morning of that day, you will:

    - Write down who you are giving the Kindness to and why
    - Put Kindness into action

3. On the evening of that day, you will:

    - Reflect on a more Kind life

Pretty straightforward, right? Being a Kind human isn't always this neat and tidy, but I hope this will be a good place to start.

Here's to less confetti and more compassion,

Houston

52

[WEEKS]

Week 1

*Don't ask yourself what the world needs, ask yourself what
makes you come alive. And then go and do that. Because
what the world needs is people who have come alive.*
—Howard Washington Thurman

MORNING

[
1 Person: Yourself
]

Why do you deserve Kindness today?

_____

_____

_____

_____

_____

_____

_____

_____

10 Minutes: Write down one thing you love about your
Past Self, one thing you love about your Present Self,
and one thing you love about your Future Self. Put it
somewhere you will see daily.

EVENING

Reflect

- Did you do it?   ☐ YES!   ☐ NOT YET

- If yes, what did you learn? If not yet, what got in the way?

Week 2

MORNING

1 Person: Yourself

Why do you deserve Kindness today?

_____

_____

_____

_____

_____

_____

_____

_____

_____

_____

**10 Minutes: Go outside and identify five things you
are grateful for that exist within a ten-minute radius of
where you live.**

EVENING

Reflect

- Did you do it?   ☐ YES!   ☐ NOT YET

- If yes, what did you learn? If not yet, what got in the way?

Week 3

Other things may change us, but we start and end with the family.
—Anthony Brandt

MORNING

1 Person: A Family Member

Who are they?

_____

_____

_____

Why do they deserve Kindness?

_____

_____

_____

What's your favorite thing about this person?

_____

_____

10 Minutes: Send a note to a family member letting them know you are going to call and intentionally leave a voice message. In the message, share one specific thing you love or admire about this person.

EVENING

Reflect

- Did you do it?   ☐ YES!   ☐ NOT YET

- If yes, what did you learn? If not yet, what got in the way?

Week 4

Nothing shakes the smiling heart.
—Santosh Kalwar

MORNING

1 Person: A Family Member

Who are they?

_____

_____

_____

Why do they deserve Kindness?

_____

_____

_____

What's your favorite thing about this person?

_____

_____

_____

10 Minutes: Send a family member a picture of your face smiling and tell them one reason they make you happy.

EVENING

Reflect

- Did you do it? ☐ YES! ☐ NOT YET

- If yes, what did you learn? If not yet, what got in the way?

Week 5

*The greatest gift of family life is to be intimately acquainted with people
you might never even introduce yourself to, had life not done it for you.*
—Kendall Hailey

MORNING

1 Person: A Family Member

Who are they?

_____

_____

Why do they deserve Kindness?

_____

_____

What's your favorite thing about this person?

_____

_____

**10 Minutes: Write a short, loving note to a family
member nearby or who you live with. Hide the note in
a place that might be hard for them to discover. Text
them throughout the day with mysterious hints and then
connect with them once they find their prize.**

EVENING

Reflect

- Did you do it? ☐ YES! ☐ NOT YET

- If yes, what did you learn? If not yet, what got in the way?

Week 6

Call it a clan, call it a network, call it a tribe, call it a family.
Whatever you call it, whoever you are, you need one.
—Jane Howard

MORNING

> **1 Person: A Family Member**

Who are they?

_____

_____

_____

Why do they deserve Kindness?

_____

_____

_____

What's your favorite thing about this person?

_____

_____

10 Minutes: Make a formal invitation to hang out with this week's chosen family member. Send them a Save the Date and commit to doing something you know they will love.

EVENING

Reflect

- Did you do it? ☐ YES! ☐ NOT YET

- If yes, what did you learn? If not yet, what got in the way?

Week 7

*The most beautiful discovery true friends make is that
they can grow separately without growing apart.*
—Elisabeth Foley

MORNING

> **1 Person: A Friend**

Who are they?

_____

_____

Why do they deserve Kindness?

_____

_____

What's your favorite thing about this person?

_____

_____

10 Minutes: Send a friend you trust three to five pictures of all your worst face angles with a caption like, "You're the only person in the world I would trust to send these to. Thanks for loving me from all angles."

EVENING

Reflect

- Did you do it? ☐ YES! ☐ NOT YET

- If yes, what did you learn? If not yet, what got in the way?

Week 8

The greatest moments in life are not concerned with selfish achievements but rather with the things we do for the people we love and esteem.
—Walt Disney

MORNING

1 Person: A Best Friend

Who are they?

_____

_____

Why do they deserve Kindness?

_____

_____

What's your favorite thing about this person?

_____

10 Minutes: Write two haikus (three-line poems with five syllables on the first line, seven syllables on the second, and five syllables on the third). One poem will just be about this person. The other poem will be about your friendship. Text your masterpieces to them or write them out and give them to your best friend.

EVENING

Reflect

- Did you do it?   ☐ YES!   ☐ NOT YET

- If yes, what did you learn? If not yet, what got in the way?

Week 9

Life is partly what we make it, and partly what
it is made by the friends we choose.
—Tennessee Williams

MORNING

[**1 Person: A Friend**]

Who are they?

_____

_____

Why do they deserve Kindness?

_____

_____

What's your favorite thing about this person?

_____

_____

**10 Minutes: Create a five-item bucket list of things you
want to do with this friend and then ask them to write
another five. Together, you will then have a "Top Ten
Friendship Bucket List" to accomplish together. Save it
somewhere important and follow through.**

EVENING

Reflect

- Did you do it?   ☐ YES!   ☐ NOT YET

- If yes, what did you learn? If not yet, what got in the way?

Week 10

Friendship is born at that moment when one person says to
another, "What! You too? I thought I was the only one."
—C.S. Lewis

MORNING

[**1 Person: A Friend**]

Who are they?

_____

_____

Why do they deserve Kindness?

_____

_____

What's your favorite thing about this person?

_____

_____

10 Minutes: Find an image, video, or quote that reminds you of this friend and send them a note explaining why this particular piece of media or inspiration is positively connected to this person in your mind.

EVENING

Reflect

- Did you do it?   ☐ YES!   ☐ NOT YET

- If yes, what did you learn? If not yet, what got in the way?

Week 11

Tell me who you walk with, and I'll tell you who you are.
—Esmeralda Santiago

MORNING

1 Person: A Person You Admire

Who are they?

Why do they deserve Kindness?

What's your favorite thing about this person?

10 Minutes: Sit down for a conversation with a person you admire (or have a phone call), having prepared two questions regarding two things you don't know about them yet. You can ask things like "Who is the most important role model in your life?" or "What is your favorite weird thing about yourself?"

EVENING

Reflect

- Did you do it?　☐ YES!　☐ NOT YET

- If yes, what did you learn? If not yet, what got in the way?

Week 12

*The universe is full of magical things patiently
waiting for our wits to grow sharper.*
—Eden Phillpotts

MORNING

1 Person: A Person Who Makes You Laugh

Who are they?

_____

_____

Why do they deserve Kindness?

_____

_____

What's your favorite thing about this person?

_____

_____

**10 Minutes: Draw a picture on a small piece of paper
that represents a funny memory you have with this
person. Deliver it or share it digitally so they can see
and reminisce on the moment and/or how delightfully
amateurish of an artist you are.**

EVENING

Reflect

- Did you do it?   ☐ YES!   ☐ NOT YET

- If yes, what did you learn? If not yet, what got in the way?

Week 13

*Just don't give up trying to do what you really want to do. Where
there is love and inspiration, I don't think you can go wrong.*
—Ella Fitzgerald

MORNING

[**1 Person: A Person Who Inspires You**]

Who are they?

_____

_____

Why do they deserve Kindness?

_____

_____

What's your favorite thing about this person?

_____

_____

**10 Minutes: Try something new today based on this
person's inspiration. Do this activity for ten minutes,
then take a picture or video or write in a journal about
your experience. Then, if possible, share with this
person how their life has inspired you to make your life
that much cooler.**

EVENING

Reflect

- Did you do it?   ☐ YES!   ☐ NOT YET

- If yes, what did you learn? If not yet, what got in the way?

Week 14

*Diversity really means becoming complete as human beings—
all of us. We learn from each other. If you're missing on that
stage, we learn less. We all need to be on that stage.*
—Juan Felipe Herrera

MORNING

[**1 Person: A Person You Disagree With**]

Who are they?

_____

_____

Why do they deserve Kindness?

_____

_____

What's your favorite thing about this person?

_____

10 Minutes: Think of a person you disagree with and
send a text or give them a call that sounds something
like this: *I know we differ in our perspective of*
_____*, but I do appreciate*
how _____ *challenges me to*
_____ *.*

EVENING

Reflect

- Did you do it? ☐ YES! ☐ NOT YET

- If yes, what did you learn? If not yet, what got in the way?

Week 15

And once the storm is over, you won't remember how you made it through, how you managed to survive. You won't even be sure, in fact, whether the storm is really over. But one thing is certain. When you come out of the storm, you won't be the same person who walked in. That's what this storm's all about.
—*Haruki Murakami*

MORNING

[**1 Person: A Person Who Has Navigated Adversity**]

Who are they?

_____

Why do they deserve Kindness?

_____

What's your favorite thing about this person?

_____

10 Minutes: Think of a person who has navigated adversity and send them some version of this message:
I know it wasn't easy for you to _____
_____. *Your strength,* _____, *and*
_____ *are just a few of the reasons I feel*
_____ *to know you. You inspire me to*
_____.

EVENING

Reflect

- Did you do it? ☐ YES! ☐ NOT YET

- If yes, what did you learn? If not yet, what got in the way?

Week 16

All human beings are my neighbors. We share the same planet.
—Ana Monnar

MORNING

1 Person: A Neighbor

Who are they?

_____

_____

Why do they deserve Kindness?

_____

_____

What's your favorite thing about this person?

_____

_____

10 Minutes: Create an IOU card that has your name, a way to contact you, and a silly offer that says you'd be willing to help with something like watching their dog, plucking some weeds, or bringing over some extra milk when they've poured cereal and realized they were out.

EVENING

Reflect

- Did you do it? ☐ YES! ☐ NOT YET

- If yes, what did you learn? If not yet, what got in the way?

Week 17

My father didn't tell me how to live; he lived, and let me watch him do it.
—Clarence Budington Kelland

MORNING

1 Person: A Role Model You Know Personally

Who are they?

_____

_____

Why do they deserve Kindness?

_____

_____

What's your favorite thing about this person?

_____

_____

10 Minutes: Give a role model to you a call and let them know these three things: (1) why your life has been made better because of them, (2) what you've learned from being around them, and (3) how you will continue to improve because of their incredible influence.

EVENING

Reflect

- Did you do it? ☐ YES! ☐ NOT YET

- If yes, what did you learn? If not yet, what got in the way?

_____

_____

_____

_____

_____

_____

_____

_____

_____

_____

_____

_____

_____

_____

_____

_____

_____

Week 18

MORNING

1 Person: A Friend

Who are they?

Why do they deserve Kindness?

What's your favorite thing about this person?

10 Minutes: Go through your old books and find one
that you think a friend would like. Write a little note on
the inside cover about why you are passing it on. If you
don't have one on hand, find an excerpt or a poem you
can print or share and write a note about why it made
you think of this friend.

EVENING

Reflect

- Did you do it? ☐ YES! ☐ NOT YET

- If yes, what did you learn? If not yet, what got in the way?

Week 19

You can make more friends in two months by becoming interested in other people than you can in two years by trying to get other people interested in you.
—*Dale Carnegie*

MORNING

1 Person: A Friend

Who are they?

Why do they deserve Kindness?

What's your favorite thing about this person?

10 Minutes: Call your friend's family and give them a secondhand compliment. Thank them for being great parents, siblings, or guardians, and show appreciation for how they helped raise such a wonderful human being.

EVENING

Reflect

- Did you do it? ☐ YES! ☐ NOT YET

- If yes, what did you learn? If not yet, what got in the way?

Week 20

Don't make friends who are comfortable to be with. Make friends who will force you to lever yourself up.
—Thomas J. Watson

MORNING

1 Person: A Friend

Who are they?

_____

_____

Why do they deserve Kindness?

_____

_____

What's your favorite thing about this person?

_____

_____

10 Minutes: Send a voice message to a friend that lasts at least two minutes and tries to capture as many good things as possible in a short period of time.

EVENING

Reflect

- Did you do it? ☐ YES! ☐ NOT YET

- If yes, what did you learn? If not yet, what got in the way?

Week 21

*Anybody can sympathize with the sufferings of a friend, but it
requires a very fine nature to sympathize with a friend's success.*
—Oscar Wilde

MORNING

[**1 Person: A Friend**]

Who are they?

_____

_____

Why do they deserve Kindness?

_____

_____

What's your favorite thing about this group?

_____

_____

**10 Minutes: Put together a small group text or email
inviting a friend to share their recent wins—big or small.
This could be as simple as flossing five days in a row
or as significant as running a big race, a promotion at
work, or a meaningful relationship milestone.**

EVENING

Reflect

- Did you do it?   ☐ YES!   ☐ NOT YET

- If yes, what did you learn? If not yet, what got in the way?

Week 22

MORNING

1 Person: A Family Member

Who are they?

_____

_____

Why do they deserve Kindness?

_____

_____

What's your favorite thing about this person?

_____

_____

10 Minutes: Write a post on social media about an extended family member and pretend it is National _____ Day (Uncle, Second Cousin, Grandma). Share why you are proud to have this person as a part of your family.

EVENING

Reflect

- Did you do it?   ☐ YES!   ☐ NOT YET

- If yes, what did you learn? If not yet, what got in the way?

Week 23

Your task is not to seek for love, but merely to seek and find all the barriers within yourself that you have built against it and embrace them.
—Rumi

MORNING

1 Person: A Family Member

Who are they?

_____

_____

_____

Why do they deserve Kindness?

_____

_____

_____

What's your favorite thing about this person?

_____

_____

10 Minutes: Go back through old photos and find a picture of you and an extended family member. Send it to them and tell them why it's a positive memory.

EVENING

Reflect

- Did you do it?   ☐ YES!   ☐ NOT YET

- If yes, what did you learn? If not yet, what got in the way?

Week 24

Go and love someone exactly as they are. And then watch how quickly they transform into the greatest, truest version of themselves. When one feels seen and appreciated in their own essence, one is instantly empowered.
—Wes Angelozzi

MORNING

> **1 Person: A Family Member**

Who are they?

_____

_____

Why do they deserve Kindness?

_____

_____

What's your favorite thing about this person?

_____

10 Minutes: Choose a family member and then think of two words that describe them well. Use these words to find at least one quote online that captures this person's essence effectively. Then, share the quote with the family member and why it relates to them.

EVENING

Reflect

- Did you do it?   ☐ YES!   ☐ NOT YET

- If yes, what did you learn? If not yet, what got in the way?

Week 25

People think Kindness is a soft, weak, submissive influence when in reality it is the most potent, persuasive force in existence.
—Richelle E. Goodrich

MORNING

> ### 1 Person: A Family Member

Who are they?

_____

_____

Why do they deserve Kindness?

_____

_____

What's your favorite thing about this person?

_____

10 Minutes: Think of a person in your family who practices Kindness well and send them some version of this message: *I am so grateful for your _____. Your Kindness has had a/an _____ effect on my life. I am _____ and _____ because of your influence.*

EVENING

Reflect

- Did you do it? ☐ YES! ☐ NOT YET

- If yes, what did you learn? If not yet, what got in the way?

Week 26

When you say "Yes" to others, make sure you are not saying "No" to yourself.
—Paulo Coelho

MORNING

> **1 Person: Yourself**

Why do you deserve Kindness today?

_____

_____

_____

_____

_____

_____

_____

_____

_____

_____

_____

10 Minutes: Challenge three friends to send you a picture of what they believe will most make you say "Awwwww."

EVENING

Reflect

Did you do it? ☐ YES! ☐ NOT YET

If yes, what did you learn? If not yet, what got in the way?

Week 27

That is what compassion does. It challenges our assumptions, our sense of self-limitation, worthlessness, of not having a place in the world, our feelings of loneliness and estrangement. These are narrow, constrictive states of mind. As we develop compassion, our hearts open.
—Sharon Salzberg

MORNING

1 Person: Yourself

Why do you deserve Kindness today?

_____

_____

_____

_____

_____

10 Minutes: On a piece of paper (or in a note on your phone), write out "See, Be, Three." Next to "See," write your favorite physical feature about yourself. Next to "Be," jot down your favorite nonphysical trait about yourself—something about who you are, not what you look like. Next to "Three," write three positive words someone might describe you with.

EVENING

Reflect

Did you do it? ☐ YES! ☐ NOT YET

If yes, what did you learn? If not yet, what got in the way?

Week 28

*I don't need a friend who changes when I change and who
nods when I nod; my shadow does that much better.*
—Plutarch

MORNING

1 Person: A Family Member

Who are they?

Why do they deserve Kindness?

What's your favorite thing about this person?

**10 Minutes: Ask a family member for feedback today.
It might sound like this: "I want to be the best *brother/
sister/son/nephew/mother* I can be to you. What is one
thing I can do that would improve our relationship?"
When inviting feedback, be sure you don't get defensive
at someone's response, or you are less likely to get
honest feedback in the future. Take one step to close
any gaps that are identified in your conversation.**

EVENING

Reflect

- Did you do it? ☐ YES! ☐ NOT YET

- If yes, what did you learn? If not yet, what got in the way?

Week 29

Memories, even your most precious ones, fade surprisingly quickly. But I don't go along with that. The memories I value most, I don't ever see them fading.
—*Kazuo Ishiguro*

MORNING

> **1 Person: A Family Member**

Who are they?

_____

_____

Why do they deserve Kindness?

_____

_____

What's your favorite thing about this person?

_____

10 Minutes: Choose a family member that one of these prompts relates to and then call or message them with how you would complete the prompt: "A memory I have with you that always makes me smile is . . ." or "Something I've always appreciated about you is . . ." or "Thank goodness you are in this family because . . ."

EVENING

Reflect

- Did you do it?   ☐ YES!   ☐ NOT YET

- If yes, what did you learn? If not yet, what got in the way?

Week 30

MORNING

1 Person: A Family Member

Who are they?

_____

_____

Why do they deserve Kindness?

_____

_____

What's your favorite thing about this person?

_____

_____

10 Minutes: Send a calendar invite to a family member
and include at least two thoughtful topics you want
to talk about in the description. Follow through with a
phone or video call.

EVENING

Reflect

Did you do it?　☐ YES!　☐ NOT YET

If yes, what did you learn? If not yet, what got in the way?

Week 31

Let us be grateful to people who make us happy, they are the charming gardeners who make our souls blossom.
—Marcel Proust

MORNING

> **1 Person: A Family Member**

Who are they?

_____

Why do they deserve Kindness?

_____

What's your favorite thing about this person?

_____

10 Minutes: Think of a family member who helped make you the person you are today and send them some version of this message: *Your* _____
challenged me to _____.
It deepened my interest in _____
and made me a _____ *person.*
Thank you, forever, for your _____
_____.

EVENING

Reflect

- Did you do it?   ☐ YES!   ☐ NOT YET

- If yes, what did you learn? If not yet, what got in the way?

Week 32

MORNING

1 Person: A Friend

Who are they?

_____

_____

Why do they deserve Kindness?

_____

_____

What's your favorite thing about this person?

_____

_____

10 Minutes: Play a song from one of your favorite musical artists. Intentionally try to connect the lyrics or the genre to a friend of yours. Send this person the song and, with it, why you thought of them in relation to this music.

EVENING

Reflect

- Did you do it? ☐ YES! ☐ NOT YET

- If yes, what did you learn? If not yet, what got in the way?

Week 33

MORNING

[**1 Person: A Friend**]

Who are they?

_____

_____

Why do they deserve Kindness?

_____

_____

What's your favorite thing about this person?

_____

_____

10 Minutes: Send an invite to celebrate a friend's fraction birthday. For example, "I know that Friday is your half birthday, and I can't wait to eat cake over FaceTime," or "Happy one-eighth birthday! Your full birthday is only 320 days away. Let's get together for muffins and celebrate this milestone."

EVENING

Reflect

- Did you do it? ☐ YES! ☐ NOT YET

- If yes, what did you learn? If not yet, what got in the way?

Week 34

*You can always tell a real friend: when you've made a fool of
yourself he doesn't feel you've done a permanent job.*
—Laurence J. Peter

MORNING

[**1 Person: A Friend**]

Who are they?

_____

Why do they deserve Kindness?

_____

What's your favorite thing about this person?

_____

**10 Minutes: Think of a friend who makes you laugh until
you cry and send them some version of this message:** *I
just wanted to remind you that nothing makes me laugh
harder than when I am around you, not even _____*
_____. Remember that time when
you _____? I still cry-laugh
thinking about it. You bring _____
and _____ to my day.

EVENING

Reflect

Did you do it?   ☐ YES!   ☐ NOT YET

If yes, what did you learn? If not yet, what got in the way?

_____

_____

_____

_____

_____

_____

_____

_____

_____

_____

_____

_____

_____

_____

_____

_____

Week 35

Sometimes being a friend means mastering the art of timing. There is a time
for silence. A time to let go and allow people to hurl themselves into their
own destiny. And a time to prepare to pick up the pieces when it's all over.
—*Octavia Butler*

MORNING

1 Person: A Friend

Who are they?

Why do they deserve Kindness?

What's your favorite thing about this person?

10 Minutes: Let a friend know you want to reserve some time to catch up with them and then send them three calendar invites to choose from to see if one of them works. Lead the charge in finding time for quality time.

EVENING

Reflect

- Did you do it?   ☐ YES!   ☐ NOT YET

- If yes, what did you learn? If not yet, what got in the way?

Week 36

MORNING

1 Person: A Local Business Owner

Who are they?

Why do they deserve Kindness?

What's your favorite thing about this person?

10 Minutes: Leave an intentionally positive and
thoughtful review of a local place that has provided you
with good food or service.

EVENING

Reflect

- Did you do it? ☐ YES! ☐ NOT YET

- If yes, what did you learn? If not yet, what got in the way?

Week 37

Kindness can become its own motive. We are made Kind by being Kind.
—Eric Hoffer

MORNING

1 Person: A Local Acquaintance

Who are they?

_____

_____

Why do they deserve Kindness?

_____

_____

What's your favorite thing about this person?

_____

10 Minutes: Exercise curiosity today with someone that you see regularly but don't know very well. Ask the person who delivers your mail about their favorite hobby. Ask the person who makes your coffee about something they are excited about right now. Ask the person at the front desk about their most recent favorite movie or television show.

EVENING

Reflect

- Did you do it?   ☐ YES!   ☐ NOT YET

- If yes, what did you learn? If not yet, what got in the way?

Week 38

When you realize how perfect everything is, you will
tilt your head back and laugh at the sky.
—A Buddhist saying

MORNING

[**1 Person: A Stranger**]

Why do people deserve Kindness?

_____

_____

_____

_____

_____

_____

_____

_____

_____

10 Minutes: Write a short, anonymous poem about why the world is beautiful and why everyone deserves Kindness, then post it in a public space.

EVENING

Reflect

Did you do it?   ☐ YES!   ☐ NOT YET

If yes, what did you learn? If not yet, what got in the way?

Week 39

Being a role model is equal parts being who you actually are and what people hope you will be.
—Meryl Streep

MORNING

1 Person: A Person You Admire

Who are they?

_____

_____

Why do they deserve Kindness?

_____

_____

What's your favorite thing about this person?

_____

_____

10 Minutes: Film a short video of yourself talking about something you've learned from a person you admire and how it's made you a better person. Send it to them directly or tag this person in the video and, if possible, send them a message with your gratitude.

EVENING

Reflect

Did you do it? ☐ YES! ☐ NOT YET

If yes, what did you learn? If not yet, what got in the way?

Week 40

Spiritual love is when you see new faces as the oldest.
—Michael Bassey Johnson

MORNING

> **1 Person: A Stranger**

Why do people deserve Kindness?

_____

_____

_____

_____

_____

_____

_____

_____

10 Minutes: Leave an intentional compliment on a receipt or napkin for someone who provided you service this week. It could be a waiter or waitress, the person who prepared your coffee, or the grocery store clerk.

EVENING

Reflect

Did you do it? ☐ YES! ☐ NOT YET

If yes, what did you learn? If not yet, what got in the way?

Week 41

We know we cannot plant seeds with closed fists.
To sow, we must open our hands.
—Adolfo Perez Esquivel

MORNING

[**1 Person: A Person Who Has Forgiven You**]

Who are they?

_____

_____

Why do they deserve Kindness?

_____

_____

What's your favorite thing about this person?

_____

**10 Minutes: Think of a person who has offered
you forgiveness and send them some version
of this message:** *Your graciousness and*
_____ *has not been forgotten.*
When you _____*, it meant a*
lot and I'm very _____ *for you.*
Thank you for _____.

EVENING

Reflect

• Did you do it? ☐ YES! ☐ NOT YET

• If yes, what did you learn? If not yet, what got in the way?

Never lose sight of the fact that the most important yardstick of your success will be how you treat people—your family, friends, and coworkers, and even strangers you meet along the way.
—Barbara Bush

MORNING

1 Person: A Coworker

Who are they?

_____

_____

Why do they deserve Kindness?

_____

_____

What's your favorite thing about this person?

_____

10 Minutes: Create a group text with some people who know your coworker and prompt everyone to share one good thing about this person to celebrate them just because.

EVENING

Reflect

- Did you do it?   ☐ YES!   ☐ NOT YET

- If yes, what did you learn? If not yet, what got in the way?

Week 43

Experience is a master teacher, even when it's not our own.
—Gina Greenlee

MORNING

1 Person: A Role Model You've Never Met

Who are they?

_____

_____

Why do they deserve Kindness?

_____

_____

What's your favorite thing about this person?

_____

_____

10 Minutes: Go back and reread or rewatch something that a role model you have never met has done or has created that inspires you. Share it with one other person so they can be inspired too!

EVENING

Reflect

Did you do it? ☐ YES! ☐ NOT YET

If yes, what did you learn? If not yet, what got in the way?

Week 44

MORNING

1 Person: An Educator

Who are they?

_____

_____

Why do they deserve Kindness?

_____

_____

What's your favorite thing about this person?

_____

10 Minutes: Find a way to contact an old educator of yours and send them a note communicating what you remember from their class and what you learned from them about work or life. If you are unable to find a contact, write a thank-you note to a local school sharing the story of the educator who impacted you.

EVENING

Reflect

- Did you do it? ☐ YES! ☐ NOT YET

- If yes, what did you learn? If not yet, what got in the way?

Week 45

If we take the widest and wisest view of a Cause, there is no such thing as a Lost Cause because there is no such thing as a Gained Cause. We fight for lost causes because we know that our defeat and dismay may be the preface to our successors' victory, though that victory itself will be temporary; we fight rather to keep something alive than in the expectation that anything will triumph.
—*T. S. Eliot*

MORNING

> **1 Person: Someone in Charge of an Organization**

What organization?

Why do they deserve Kindness?

What's your favorite thing about this organization?

10 Minutes: Research more deeply an organization that means something to you. If you have the ability, write an email to the person who runs it (or started it) and explain why you believe in their work. If you can, give a donation.

EVENING

Reflect

- Did you do it? ☐ YES! ☐ NOT YET

- If yes, what did you learn? If not yet, what got in the way?

Week 46

And what is it to work with love?
It is to weave the cloth with threads drawn from your heart,
even as if your beloved were to wear that cloth.
It is to build a house with affection, even as if your
beloved were to dwell in that house.
It is to sow seeds with tenderness and reap the harvest with
joy, even as if your beloved were to eat the fruit.
It is to charge all things you fashion with a breath of your own spirit,
And to know that all the blessed dead are standing about you and watching.
—*Kahlil Gibran*

MORNING

1 Person: An Acquaintance

Who are they?

_____

_____

Why do they deserve Kindness?

_____

_____

What's your favorite thing about this person?

_____

10 Minutes: Write a thank-you note to a delivery person, a garbage collector, or someone else who visits your home regularly, letting them know you are grateful for their consistent service and for the care they bring to their work.

EVENING

Reflect

- Did you do it? ☐ YES! ☐ NOT YET

- If yes, what did you learn? If not yet, what got in the way?

Week 47

Never doubt that a small group of thoughtful, committed citizens
can change the world. Indeed, it is the only thing that ever has.
—Margaret Mead

MORNING

1 Person: A Friend

Who are they?

_____

_____

Why do they deserve Kindness?

_____

_____

What's your favorite thing about this person?

_____

**10 Minutes: Think of a friend who shows expertise in
their work and send them some version of this message:**
*I just wanted to let you know I am grateful for your
expertise in* _____ .
It inspires me and _____ .
I love how it provides _____
to people.

100 • BE KIND

EVENING

Reflect

- Did you do it? ☐ YES! ☐ NOT YET

- If yes, what did you learn? If not yet, what got in the way?

Week 48

Language creates reality. Words have power. Speak always to create joy.
—Deepak Chopra

MORNING

> **1 Person: A Friend**

Who are they?

_____

_____

Why do they deserve Kindness?

_____

_____

What's your favorite thing about this person?

_____

10 Minutes: Collaborate with a friend to start a text message thread that includes another friend. Exchange positive messages back and forth about this third friend as if you didn't know you included them in the thread. Pretend it's "positive gossiping" that the person can accidentally see.

EVENING

Reflect

- Did you do it? ☐ YES! ☐ NOT YET

- If yes, what did you learn? If not yet, what got in the way?

Week 49

In life, it is never the big battle, the big moment, the big speech,
the big election. That does not change things. What changes things
is every day, getting up and rendering small acts of service and
love beyond that what's expected of you or required of you.
—Cory Booker

MORNING

1 Person: A Family Member

Who are they?

Why do they deserve Kindness?

What's your favorite thing about this person?

10 Minutes: Create a homemade or digital coupon good for one specific chore and send it to a family member who would appreciate it. For example, "This coupon is good for one snow shoveling," or "This ticket is valid for one grill cleaning." Let them know when or how they can redeem this act of service.

EVENING

Reflect

Did you do it?   ☐ YES!   ☐ NOT YET

If yes, what did you learn? If not yet, what got in the way?

Week 50

Scared is what you're feeling. Brave is what you're doing.
—Emma Donoghue

MORNING

1 Person: A Family Member

Who are they?

_____

_____

Why do they deserve Kindness?

_____

_____

What's your favorite thing about this person?

_____

10 Minutes: Think of a family member who is brave and send them some version of this message: *Superheroes have costumes, but you don't need a cape or mask to be _____. That time when you _____ inspired me because _____. Thank you for your bravery in this world.*

EVENING

Reflect

Did you do it? ☐ YES! ☐ NOT YET

If yes, what did you learn? If not yet, what got in the way?

Week 51

For beautiful eyes, look for the good in others; for beautiful lips, speak only words of Kindness; and for poise, walk with the knowledge that you are never alone.
—Audrey Hepburn

MORNING

1 Person: Yourself

Why do you deserve Kindness?

_____

_____

_____

_____

_____

_____

_____

10 Minutes: Send a message to two or three close friends and request their Kindness. Ask them if they would share with you a positive memory from your time together as friends.

EVENING

Reflect

- Did you do it? ☐ YES! ☐ NOT YET

- If yes, what did you learn? If not yet, what got in the way?

Week 52

We are not human beings, we are human becomings.
—John Addison

MORNING

[**1 Person: Yourself**]

Why do you deserve Kindness?

_____

_____

_____

_____

_____

_____

_____

10 Minutes: Write down a list of your three favorite moments over the last year and put it in a place to remind yourself of the power of Kindness. Make it look nice so you can stare at it often and post it proudly. Share this list with someone you care about and tell them they would be really good at this whole Year of Kindness thing.

EVENING

Reflect

- Did you do it? ☐ YES! ☐ NOT YET

- If yes, what did you learn? If not yet, what got in the way?

ou finished! Or, perhaps, you're just getting started.

The world needs us to prioritize Kindness in our daily lives. Every day we have the ability to practice being Kind until, slowly, we start to *become* it. Kindness will never be commonplace in our communities until it is habitual in our hearts.

So, let's get to work.

Houston

BIBLIOGRAPHY

FURTHER READING

Borba, Michele. *UnSelfie: Why Empathetic Kids Succeed in Our All-About-Me World*. New York: Touchstone, 2016.

Brown, Brené. *Rising Strong: How the Ability to Reset Transforms the Way We Live, Love, Parent, and Lead*. New York: Spiegel & Grau, 2015.

Cain, Susan. *Quiet: The Power of Introverts in a World That Can't Stop Talking*. New York: Crown Publishers, 2012.

Duhigg, Charles. *The Power of Habit: Why We Do What We Do in Life and Business*. New York: Random House, 2012.

Frankl, Viktor E. *Man's Search for Meaning: An Introduction to Logotherapy*. Boston: Beacon Press, 1962.

Krznaric, Roman. *Empathy: Why It Matters, and How to Get It*. London: Rider Books, 2015.

Salzberg, Sharon. *Lovingkindness: The Revolutionary Art of Happiness*. Boulder, CO: Shambhala, 2018.

School of Life. *On Being Nice: A Guide to Friendship and Connection*. London: The School of Life, 2022.

School of Life. *The School of Life: An Emotional Education*. London: The School of Life, 2019.

Zaki, Jamil. *The War for Kindness: Building Empathy in a Fractured World*. New York: Crown Publishers, 2019.

Houston Kraft has dedicated nearly two decades to the pursuit of a more Kind world. He started a club focused on Kindness in high school and organized a group to help create more compassion in college. He began speaking at schools and organizations in 2009 and has presented at more than 600 events internationally.

In 2016, he cofounded CharacterStrong, which currently serves 10,000 schools across fifty states and thirty-six countries. CharacterStrong is dedicated to creating a more loving world through education and provides curricula PK–12th grade that teach skills like empathy, emotional intelligence, and Kindness.

In 2019, his face was featured on Lays BBQ chip bags as someone who helps "spread smiles." In 2020, his first book, *Deep Kindness: A Revolutionary Guide for the Way We Think, Talk, and Act in Kindness* was published by Simon & Schuster.

He has been featured on *Good Morning America*, CNN, Hallmark, Katie Couric Media, and more as an expert on developing a more empathetic, Kind world. His mom is his hero and her best life lesson is to "hug like you mean it." He lives in Venice, California, with his best friends and loves to dance, go on adventures, and build community.